This Marriage of Man the Maker and Mother Nature

The Complete Coagula Poems
Volume 2

GERALD LOCKLIN

THIS MARRIAGE OF MAN THE MAKER AND MOTHER NATURE
By Gerald Locklin

Copyright © 2014 by Coagula Publications – a division of Flechaverde, Inc.
All rights reserved.

ISBN 13: 978-1499677430

This book may not be reproduced in whole or in part or in any form or format without the written permission of Gerald Locklin or his representative.

Published by: Flechaverde, Inc.
P.O. Box 5228 , Huntington Park, CA 90255
1-424-2-COAGULA
www. coagula. com • 88gallery @gmail. com

Coagula Art Journal Issue #111, November, 2014

Copyright ©1992, 2014 by Flechaverde Inc.
All Rights Reserved

Coagula Art Journal is published on occasion by Flechaverde, Inc who is solely responsible for its contents. However, any opinions expressed within the fair confines of *Coagula Art Journal* do not necessarily represent the views or policies of this journal, its owner (Flechaverde, Inc.), or any of his agents, staff, employees, members, interns, volunteers, retailers, distributors or distribution venues.

Bylined articles and editorials represent the views of their authors. Unattributed editorials are the opinion of the editor at the time of their composition.

All correspondence (email included) becomes the property of the publisher and cannot be returned (or erased). We retain the right to accept or reject all correspondence, in any form, primarily but not exclusively for purposes of publication.

Coagula Art Journal retains the right to reject any advertising and to adjust advertising rates on any basis without any notice. We are not responsible for any claims made by our advertisers.

Coagula Art Journal is distributed manually, electronically and in formats that might be spontaneously embraced. Placement in a locale in no way implies an entity's sponsorship of, liability for or attachment to this journal. Distribution location maintains the right to distribute this publication for the price it chooses—for purposes of import duties and value assessed each issue, the wholesale price of one copy is $3.00

DEDICATION

The author would like to dedicates this book to
Todd Fox, Wendy Rainey, Adrienne Foon and Ronald Burras.

ACKNOWLEDGMENTS

This book was made possible by the efforts of many people. Over the years, publishing *Coagula Art Journal* was a process involving dozens of people, without whom these poems would not have seen the light of day in the nationally distributed free art magazine.

This volume owes thanks to Bryan Chagolla for data entry, Tom Callinan for sharp editing and style decisions, and to Eric Minh-Swenson for the cover photo of the author, taken while the author was reading selections from *You Need Never Look Out a Window*, Volume 1 of his Complete Coagula Poems at the book's outdoor pig roast release party.

I

ART IN LIFE

the anti-expert

i've written hundreds of art poems
and quite a few jazz poems too,
and i'm beginning to branch out
into photography and architecture
poems.

frankly i consider some of these poems
nothing short of supercalifragilistic,

and i bet they'd be a lot less
stimulating if i had any effing idea
what i was talking about.

GERALD LOCKLIN

Robert Graves Left England for Mallorca

I never cared much for the art of Bruce Nauman,
As I am sufficiently Old School to resent
The Cults of Ugliness and Diminishment.

But my opinion was instantaneously altered
Upon reading in *The New Yorker*
That he and Susan Rothenberg
"go into Santa Fe now and then,
But they steer clear of
The thriving art colony."

Why have we not learned from history
That the individual must shun,
To the extent possible,
Involvement with Collectivists?

who took the bite out of the apple?

on the back cover
of *the new yorker*,
john and yoko are sitting up
in bed, crosslegged, holding
flowers and hawking computers.

the ad is captioned
"think different."

i don't have anything
against advertisements.
hemingway did them.
i'd do them if anyone asked
(hint, hint).
i hope my publishers will place
a whole shitload of them.

but i don't talk about karma;
i don't pretend to be unconventional;
i wouldn't marry yoko ono
if she were the last piece of ass on earth

and i hope my ad reads
"think grammatically."

their godmother

hadn't and haven't the conceptual artists
ever heard of gertrude stein?

in *tender buttons* (1914) she was already
liberating their signifiers from their
signifieds,
using words for their own sake,
the sight and sound of them,
without any necessary connection to
referents in the "real" (external or mental)
world, by analogy to the way in which
abstract/non-representational artists
employ line and color.

in the *making of americans* (written 1906-08),
she was already treating human personality and
character in fiction as the habitual repetition of
behavioral traits, while employing an imitative
style of serial-repetitive prose to ratchet
the idea home.

her "portraits" (e.g. of cezanne, matisse, picasso,
and mabel dodge) utilized cubistic multiple
perspective and futuristic multiple images,
as did melanctha (one of her earliest portrayals
of a bisexual black woman) and other "lives."

in her works in general (except for the anecdotal,
such as the autobiography of alice b. toklas and
her memoirs of occupied and liberated france),
the grasping of the concept obviates the need to
experience the entire text: i'd guess fewer readers
have made it through the *making of americans* than
through *finnegans wake*.

and the infamous but beautiful "pigeons on the grass alas" passage from *four saints in three acts* (1929) strikes me as the exploration of a non-repetitive number (syllable) series deconstructing grammar and aspiring to the freest form: one not reducible to pattern.

how can i get excited when later, lesser minds arrive with such less charm at destinations she departed from decades ahead of them?

american art at the end of the millennium

elvis presley pulled out his six-shooter,
struck a manly pose,
and shot andy warhol.
there were many elvises
but only one andy.
thus, the elvises shot andy
many times.
andy went down gracefully,
as might be expected,
and with dignity,
his trademark white wig
undisturbed.

then elvis shot jackson pollock.
it didn't matter that jackson
was dead, elvis shot him anyway,
many times. jackson just smiled
and swigged another,
straight from the bottle,
though riddled like dick tracy.

elvis tracked robert smithson
along a spiral path
to the end of a jetty.
there he shot him.
many times.
robert just sort of tipped over
into the great salt lake.
the trillions of sand fleas
were at first angered,
then settled down to their version
of a thanksgiving feast.

finally elvis shot jeff koons' metallic
rabbit.
but since the bunny was
the very emblem of postmodern reflexivity,
the bullet was deflected back into
the brain of elvis.
(actually the bullet was larger than
the brain of elvis,
though smaller than his liver.)
that was it for elvis.

that was it for pop culture.
as high culture at least.
pop culture was once again pop culture.

thus, with elvis out of the way,
the artist of the new millennium
was freed to do something different
from what art had been doing,
maybe even something as radically different
as what artists used to do,
back when they were expected to do things
most people couldn't.

I Have No Regrets Concerning Edith Piaf

Yes, she was an icon to the French,
And an inspiration to all of us,
A Sparrow of the streets,
A woman of the people,
A heroine to the poor,
A war hero,
A flouter of convention and authority,
A possessor of an inimitable voice,
Of an indelibly patented style,

Who did indeed age and die
All too sadly before her time,

But, you know, like any addict,
She also seems to have been,
A royal pain in the ass
To an awful lot of people,

So yes, I'll never tire
Of listening to her,

But no, I'm just as glad
I never had a chance
To meet her,
Let alone (God forbid)
Work for her.

**tarnishing their reputation
1999**

gunning down pre-schoolers
gives a bad name
to the lunatic fringe.

david parlato

i record a couple of poems
with his bass accompaniment
among friends in the living room
of the albuquerque home
of mark weber and janet simon,

and we move easily together
over the words and notes,
no arranged signals,
just my slightest nod or inflection
to key him into mood forays
that i trust will be as enlightening
to listeners as they are to me.

later, i insist on singing
(well, sort of)
weill's "september song" in front of david's heroic
attempts to mitigate my vocal shortcomings,

and then i just sit down to watch and listen as
he does his own things with a standard or two,
and, you know, i've heard a lot
of the best-known bass players
at l.a.'s jazz bakery and the carpenter center
on our campus
but none ever struck me as more at ease with
his instrument than david,
and many seemed a good deal less.
his fingers move along the strings
as mine do, on a good day, over a poem;
his are happy with the music they are making,
as i on such days am with mine.

THIS MARRIAGE OF MAN THE MAKER AND MOTHER NATURE

i think his is the even more perpetual and
intimate of relationships with his art, though
mine is too subject to distractions,
interruptions, the anxiety of failure,
the need to inscribe, make permanent.
i always wanted to be able to do at the piano
what he does with acoustic, standing bass,
but i did not possess the gift for it,
the natural affinity,
that special brand of indefinable intelligence,
that unit of mind and flesh and weapon.
thus i am all the more equipped
to understand the neurological miracle involved
in david's doing,
and i am humbled by it
as i angrily attempt to force the music
that i vaguely hear in my imagination
into the casings of my sausage sentences,

this recitative, for instance,
of sharing an evening of the life in music
of the consummate professional who remains
the inveterate mozartian amateur,
living the life of music out of love of it,
at one with his instinct, his calling,
himself.

GERALD LOCKLIN

enigma variations:
the sculpture of john frame, 1980-2005,
Long Beach Museum of Art

the marriage of the junkyard and
the redwood grove,
of craft and luck,
chaos and calculation,
blake, skeleton, cocteau,
the nightmare and the reverie,
the quick and revenant,
the sea and ahab/moby/ishmael,
the universal search for personality
and how to lose it,
the licking flames of heaven and
the colorless and silent conflagration
that is something else.
birth, purgatory, death.
the commedia del arte and unamuno's
tragic sense of life,
appropriation of the macrocosmic wilderness
and the legible illumination of a splinter,
assemblage of the sundial, skull, and
elevator indicator,
the hermit as extrovert,
the introspection of alice,
memento your vita,
calligraphy of the peripheral,
the peritoneal,
lightning fueled by propane,
the oxyacetylene conception,
god needs no eyes to see,

THIS MARRIAGE OF MAN THE MAKER AND MOTHER NATURE

a simian may though untrained eloquently
declaim hamlet,
all that we need to know we
knew before knowledge,
silver and gold, lead and feathers,
man is loved by the maker, the
mad molecule,
sebastian was the master archer,
balance/focus, hocus/pocus,
hoc est enim corpus meum,
and this grail is my blood,
the artist goes where he goes,
he follows his nose,
the good man knows not if it shows,
the ultimate assembling is not an assembly line,
it is one of a kind.

aside from my being an ignoramus,
why hadn't i heard of this guy?
isn't what emerges from his crucible of
elementals more original and well made than
the replications of the fashionable?

by implication, these works indict egos in
dread of extinction.

bergamot station: 10-28-00

what a joke:
call yourself an artist,
produce a bunch of unoriginal
and aesthetically unpleasing artefacts
that anyone would have to be an idiot
or masochist to dole out legitimately
earned money for, and then complain
that our society does not support
our artists. notice that it does
support its architects, the best at
least, quite well, but then again to
be an architect requires a great deal
of knowledge, education (formal or
self-taught), and plain hard work/
long hours—less time for sitting
around smoking dope and sopping up
pop culture on the telly.

russell crotty has an installation
in an enormous room, a few big balls
hanging from the ceiling. since space
in our society is at a premium, if i
were rich i'd buy the room, puncture
the balloons, and keep the empty space
as a sort of comfort, like the wildernesses
that i never get to but am reassured of
something simply knowing that they're there.

again, if i were rich and could afford
a house with real big rooms, i'd buy
the oversized wooden furnishings
in the gallery of functional art--
elongated benches that, it is suggested,
might have been the salvage of odysseus'
vessel--and i'd bring them home because
i like big things that won't break easily.
i'd throw a party and let my friends sit
on my newly acquired objets d'art and

soak the wood with cheap red wine i'd
be providing--which would probably be no
worse than what the ancients filled their
wineskins with--or bullfight fans today.
i'd at least know that i'd gotten for
my money a place to park my butt:
no rich fool am i!

most of all i have to laugh at
the signs that warn of constant
"closed circuit surveillance."
and the way the gallery attendants follow
me around. do i look dumb enough
to steal this stuff?! is this entire scene
somehow predicated on tax write offs?
am i missing the point?

good photos by lewis morley, though:
christine keeler, beyond the fringe,
and two enormously titted birds
at a table across from suits
in london's first topless club.

(photographers are such wonderfully
shameless fetishists...but i'd have
also opened a bottomless club,
the women only clothed from the waist up.)

and who'd have ever guessed
dame judi dench
was once a vixen?

christian heeb: south Kensington, photo, 2000

borough of continuous town houses
and hotels. city of crescents.

borough of endless reconstruction,
or circulating traffic,
circumambulating citizens,
of brick, of layers of live above/
below the level of the thoroughfares.
of souls in transit.

borough of signals cruelly,
sometimes sadistically mixed that
send in opposite directions two
who might have made a sympathetic
life together, instead condemned
to the emotional terrain of
thomas hardy.

**BUT PLEASE: NO
THOMAS KINKADES**

because i write a lot of jazz poems,
people here and abroad often send me
CDs that they've enjoyed and think
that i might, and they're usually correct.

i certainly do not expect such gifts,
but i appreciate the kindnesses.

i also write a lot of art poems but so far
i have received no rembrandts.

robert polidori: photo of the l.v.m.h. building

we need buildings whose planes
and edges and relationships
surprise us, remind us that

the human possibilities
have not been exhausted.

II

THE POSTMODERN

sigmar polke:
nixon and kruschev as potato heads

the satirists had a field day
with richard nixon

but, in his grave,
he enjoys the last laugh:

he was such an easy target
that their rapiers
became as blunt as bludgeons
and never quite regained their edge.

Douglas Gordon: the searchers, video installation, 1999-2004

i'm naïve enough
to still be suspicious of
the postmodernist works that simply
recontextualize classic predecessors,
landmarks of our culture/Culture.
i'd like to see a little demonstration
of skill, of execution,
on the part of the artist,
as we had early-on by picasso and warhol,
to go along with the conceptualization.
i know i've practiced metafiction,
metapoetry, myself, but i don't
consider that a contradiction.
i don't consider myself a philistine either,
just someone who,
like the general run of humanity,
hungers and thirsts for an art that
does not turn its nose up at our desire for
beauty, for objects of aesthetic contemplation.

still, if i had to be subjected to
scenes from a movie
projected day and night
for the next five years
in a spacious downtown gallery
windowed on all sides,

i would much rather have my senses
saturated with the monumental myths and
mesas of the visionary, passionate,
craftsmanly, and quintessentially american
john ford,

than with, say *pink flamingos*,
warhol's *frankenstein, eraserhead*,
or *greaser's palace*.

karen carson:
***untitled*, 1971, cotton duck and industrial zippers**

this is supposed to make
a feminist statement,

and i would say that it makes
a very graphic and effective one,

because it looks to me as if
the cotton duck has got
his dick caught in one of the
industrial zippers.

cindy sherman

i remember a woman
back in graduate school
who loved to throw costume parties
because she could dress up in, say,
a tiger skin, and show off
her shapely body while cosmeticizing
and distracting from her somewhat
blemished countenance.

after all, it was all in good fun.

so, sure, we've heard about
"the destructive effects of the male gaze"
until, we're, well, cyanidal in the face, but
in the "untitled film stills,"
and other early "untitleds,"
isn't there more than a smidgeon
of narcissism, of exhibitionism,
of feminism once again wanting
to have it both ways?

and in the later crude and brutal
meat—like posturings, is what
we're seeing really what the
voyeuristic male does to the woman's
image of herself,

or the simple ravagings wrought on
a woman's beauty by the indifferent
timebomb within the *dna*?

s/he who lives by self-love
dies in loathing.

edward ruscha
US, 1995

we are us, and we are the u.s.,
the u.s.a., the letters shadowy
behind the sprigs of grain,
the urban wheat,

and i don't care
what ruscha meant
or thought he meant
or if he, badly, or slyly, meant
to mean nothing

jake and dinos chapman: *zygotic acceleration, biogenetic, de-sublimated libidinal model*, 1995

the penile noses and the anal mouths
of these adolescent girls all joined beneath
a continuous torso are not especially
attractive features,

but we applaud their multicultural diversity

and their impeccably-imperially good taste
in jogging shoes and designer coiffures.

LOUISE BOURGEOISE: *SELF-PORTRAIT*, 2001

mainly a matter of holes
and of intestinal tubes
between the holes.
squatting.
a self-perpetuating organism.
some stringy hair
and eyes not entirely unintelligent. a sail boat
for a heart: thus, not devoid
of romanticism.
not much in the way of beauty,
though.

i don't encourage illusions,
but i could never portray
a woman in such a clinical,
anatomical, functional way.
they are just too beautiful to
me, and the contemplation
of their loveliness is one of life's
few basic and enduring joys.
i suppose she would blame men for this.

time you get your head straight,
lady, ladies, and it's something
i can't do for you.

david hammons:
***concerto in black and blue*, 2002**

the new yorker says the installation
celebrates
"the beauty of nothingness."
and there *is* beauty to
this photo of the corridors.

the problem is that we are seeing
not nothingness
but blues and blacks and whites,
walls and floors and ceiling.
we see four humans--
none of them the artist--
and the woman in stylish contemplation
looks pretty darn good to me.
and what is that zigging-zagging bolt of
electricity in front of her--an aura?
a cognitive-emotional charge?

nothingness may well be beautiful
but none of us will find out in this life.

elizabeth murray:
bop

how we loved the cartoon shows
(not on t.v. but in movie theatres),
especially the holiday buffets
of twenty-five selections.
we had our favorites, though:
mighty mouse and donald duck,
tom and jerry, popeye,
bugs, the road runner...
and we greeted them with gasps
of gratified desire.
the popularity of mickey mouse
was a myth,
and god knew what he saw in
skinny minnie.
while all attempts at education,
short of *fantasia*, were met with
catcalls, boos, and yawns,
we marked the days of
expectation leading to
such smorgasbords
of narrative delights,
and experienced a letdown close
to clinical depression as we filed
out of the movie palace.
to be kept home from such
a superbowl of cherries would have been a felony
of parenting
admitting no pardon.

so how today do i greet this
syntactless appropriation of the
lexicon of our unmediated
prelapsarian nostalgia?

BOO, HISS, YAWN!!!

the super-ego and the id

on the same day that i read
how the political ladies of vegas
have launched a hell-bent campaign
to rid sin city of such outmoded embarrassments
as call girls, chorus girls, and skimpily attired
cocktail waitresses,

i open my *new yorker* to an art-review
of matthew barney's *cremaster 3,*
filmed within the double helix guggenheim,
where leggy, white-gloved, silver-wigged-and-
sandaled models pose in pasties and bejeweled
g-strings, and a catwoman upon a pedestal
bares claws...in fact bares all.

if this be satire,
then let's satirize the hell out of them.

sigmar polke:
the ride on the eight of infinity, II

a great deal of postmodernism glorifies
popular culture not by recontextualization
but by comparison with itself.

I can only conceive of ever again
visiting disneyland
or any theme park
if the alternative were an exhibition
of works such as this.

GERALD LOCKLIN

III

Jean-Michel Basquiat

Kinship

In the 1980s he employed collage,
Re-contextualization, ekpharsis,
Mixing of the levels of discourse,
Juxtaposition of high and pop cultures,
Improvisation, truncation, quotation,
Symbols, metaphors, and fun,
A sense of play, of freedom.

I was employing these techniques
In the same spirit in the 1960s and
1970s, but you can be sure he did not
Learn them from me because he was no
Doubt as unaware of anything I was doing
As were all but a very few of the billions
Of people on Planet Earth (not that I had
Avid readers on some other planet).

It was all just part of the zeitgeist;
It was all just in the air.
It must have felt good to him.
It sure felt good to me.

Still does.

Starting with Basquiat

He frequently used as his starting point
A book.

I frequently launch my poems
From a painting.

'Nuff Said

Simple Truths resided in
His pithy, witty, titles:

e.g., *The Irony of the Black Cop,
Per Capita, Obnoxious Liberals,*
And my personal favorite,
Skin Head Wig.

I also enjoyed the incidental way
He inconspicuously juxtaposed
"Toilet" and "Bank"

Three Interesting Questions

1. Was Basquiat in a Class with Andy Warhol?
2. Was Andy in a Class with Basquiat?
3. What color is your brain?

Primitives

In the video interview
The erstwhile graffiti artist,
Occasionally seemingly guilty
Of spraypainted solecisms and
Misspellings, proves to be intelligent,
Literate, literary, articulate, disciplined,
Civil, cooperative, and sober:

Well educated, well trained, and well groomed,

And mindful of the undiscovered geniuses
Of the Mississippi Delta, who never made it
Upstream from their South to Soho,

Whose "native woodnotes wild" were
Warbled to the wind.

Riddle Me This Batman, 1987

Do you recognize the allusion?

I hear echoes of "Latin me that, my trinity scholard,
Out of eure sanscreed into oure eryan!"

From the last page of the Anna Livia Plurabelle
Section of Finnegans Wake.

If perchance Basquiat knew his Joyce
As well or better than
You or I, then who exactly is

The greater sophisticate?

***Pegasus*, 1987**

If he had lived to my age
He would have needed
Sherlock Holmes' magnifying glass

To decipher his own diminutive,
Hierophantic, repetitive
Hieroglyphics.

Basquiat The Film

1.

Why did he kill himself?
Why did I for thirty years fill
My consciousness with alcohol?

Regrets? As Sinatra sings,
"I've had a few, but then again,
Too few to mention."

I wonder if Basquiat regrets being dead?
Did Siddhartha indulge
In nostalgia or eternity?
Does the Buddha dig Sinatra?

Then again...Hemingway, Capote,
Marilyn Monroe...I always suspect
Foul play when someone knows too much,
Ends up unable to blab it, and I doubt you'll find
Anyone in law enforcement who, off the record,
Would label such suspicions paranoia.

2.

Cameos?
Those seen or heard or alluded to in the film
Include David Bowie/Andy Warhol,
Christopher Walken,
Dennis Hopper, Tom Waits, Miles Davis,
Bird, Diz, Iggy, Dylan, Van Morrison...

Faces and Voices of an Age of Bytes and
Facades...

3.

Dead at 27.
Prematurely? Or mature before his time.
Was John Keats immature?
I used to think so.
Now I am less sure.

But what might Basquiat have painted
If he'd lived to my age, nearly 65?
His house? Or would he have preferred
Wallpaper?

He painted the paintings he was meant to paint.
He didn't paint the ones he wasn't.
And maybe what he would have painted,
Others have, or written. And maybe what we
Write will be the fodder for some future
Basquiat? (False modesty is not humility.)

Portrait of the Artist as a Young Derelict

Basquiat, Plath, Thomas, Van Gogh, Keats:

I don't think early death was necessary
To their art.

There are other ways, those of Yeats,
Picasso, Shakespeare, Stein, Bukowski.

What *is* essential to the art of the
Sprinters and the marathoners alike.

Is the Tragic or the Comic Sense of Life.

Royalty

His heroes, saints, and kings,
Were usually black
And included Bird, Miles, Diz,
Ellington and Basie,
Joe Louis and John Lewis,
Sugar Ray Robinson (I don't
Know about Leonard),
Billie, Fats, Max, and King
Pleasure. Real kings crop
Up sometimes, but not necessarily
Crowned or haloed, or if so,
Perhaps ironically.

All the aforementioned black
Heroes have been mine also.

He also portrayed Da Vinci's
"greatest hits."

I'll have to study that one more closely
For hints to breaking the code.

LIKING ORNITHOLOGY

you know, maybe basquiat
just liked the words:
*diz, bird, ornithology,
alchemy, soap*...others—
larynx, teeth—are crossed out.
and maybe he just liked the way
that parker and gillespie looked on
album covers, posters, whatever.
all these sights and sounds vaulting
around in his skull and then looking
so nice against a black background,
a metonymic arrangement of items
related by contiguity along the
syntagmatic axis upon a pure surface.
and (thank you, susan sontag, for an
insight that's remained operable into
a fifth decade) another defeat for
interpretation.

i bet he didn't know shit about be-bop,
probably preferred reggae, disco, punk—
the music of the clubs that andy loved.

that's fine: i like words, veneers, and
faces also. i liked the idea of bird having
composed a piece called *ornithology* long
before i could have identified the piece
on hearing it. now i like to listen to
ornithology and to look at basquiat's also.

also, a true post modernist (though suspecting
the era to be a valley between the mountain
of modernism and whatever may come next),
i have no intention of researching basquiat's
actual taste in music. too lazy: i
specialize in the semi-educated guess.

THIS MARRIAGE OF MAN THE MAKER AND MOTHER NATURE

and anyway, what you saw and heard in
postmodern was generally what
you got.

yes, i not only know what i like, but
i even have a few half-assed notions
of why i like it.

GERALD LOCKLIN

IV

David Hockney

Hockney's Tulips

Tulips abound in his work.
Puns abound in Freud's case histories.

And as with those of Kertész
They seem both phallic stalk/head
And vaginal cup.

In fact, one of my Kertész notecards
Has such a drooping bloom,
Almost to the table,
That I'm afraid to send it to male friends,
Who may take it as a affront to their potency,

And to women who might take it as
A lame advertisement for mine.

Beverly Hills House Wife, 1966

He certainly never flatters the rich,
Nor the powers of the art world;
If anything he errs on the side
Of caricature,

Probably, as a child of Yorkshire,
The stern North,
A hidden part of him has always hated them,
Despised their sterile luxuries,
And, like Hemingway,
Feared he'd be corrupted by their indolence,

Even as the rest of him
Valued their patronage
And appreciated their taste and classiness
And overall good-naturedness
And good will towards him.

But genius is itself a powerful force.
The later Hemingway,
Not fabulously wealthy, but well enough off
To afford the things he enjoyed,
Wrote much better, start to finish,
Than he is generally
Given credit for by the envious,
And by those who have never had the courage
To venture an opinion of their own.
He definitely wrote better,
Start to finish,
Than any of his detractors.

And to this inexpert eye,
Hockney still seems to be
At the top of his game.

THIS MARRIAGE OF MAN THE MAKER AND MOTHER NATURE

Does it Make One Gay On the Spot

To be Painted by David Hockney?

Christopher Isherwood and Don Bachardy, 1968

On the table in front of them is placed
A bowl of fruit, topped by a
Very pointy banana.

In one easy chair
Isherwood looks at ease with himself
And with his surroundings.
From the other Bachardy
Stares at his partner,
Angry and tense.

Bachardy's legs are crossed
In the masculine manner.
Isherwood's knees are parted.

The stack of four books in front of Isherwood
Is taller, wider, and more colorful
Than Bachardy's three less-thick grey-paged
volumes.

In the foreground lies a stalk
Of Indian corn.

THIS MARRIAGE OF MAN THE MAKER AND MOTHER NATURE

Henry Geldzahler and Christopher Scott, 1969

The wall caption describes Christopher
As seeming either to have just arrived
Or to be just departing.

But to me he seems stationary
And expressionless,
A cardboard cutout,
Immobile as statuary,

Never going anywhere.

Gregory Leaning Nude, 1975

He reminds me of Michaelangelo's *David*
In three respects:

He's naked,
Has curly hair,

And a pint-sized dick.

Celia Birtwell and Mum

Hockney had fewer female muses
Than even Warhol.
Maybe only Celia and his Mum.
Apparently they were all he really needed.
Both seem to have been steadfast in their love,
How lucky for him to have had them.

And how lucky for them,
So different from each other in their qualities,
To have had their images and inner lives
Suggested into immortality
By his brilliant hand, eye, and insight.

Celia in a Black Slip Reclining 1973,
And
Celia in a Negligee, 1973

Probably because of her profile and poses,
She reminds me of Modigliani's nudes,

Except that, being partially clothed,
She's even sexier.

Divine, 1979

From the squiggly curtain,
Striped robe,
The sultanic pajamas,
And the multitude of
Riviera colors,

I'd guess that for this painting
Hockney turned into Matisse.

GERALD LOCKLIN

Christopher Without His Glasses On, 1984

Considering that Isherwood apparently
Proffered the younger Hockney
Financial aid and moral support,

I'd suggest re-titling this piece
Of grotesquerie,

No Good Deed Ever Goes Unpunished
(or Under-priced).

Portraits of Mum

I think a part of her
Loved even more,
And was even more loved by,
Son than husband.

John Fitzherbert, 1990

He could play a Lawrence gamekeeper
Or
A Forster gardener.

Dog Painting 30

Thirty too many.

Lindy Dufferin I, 2002

Women
In Tennies
Don't interest me.

The Photographer and His Daughter, 2005

She's asserting her independence
(a little obviously, awkwardly,
 as one does at that age),

And he's doing his best
To seem oblivious of

Her nubile physical beauty.

V

POP

jeff koons: *loopy*, 1999

i can't respect an artist
who would make fun of
a spoonful of marshmallow
topped by an enormous,
foregrounded maraschino
cherry.

he must have had
a fucked-up childhood.

GERALD LOCKLIN

ANDY WARHOL:
TWO MARILYNS, 1962

he shouldn't have made her face ugly,
and the face on the right even
nastier than the other,
the lips more purple,
the chin more a wedge,
half the face more blackened,
like cajun redfish,
half the hair less blonde,
fewer teeth visible,
the other eye even droopier.

montgomery clift said she had bad legs
by the making of *The Misfits*,
but she didn't have a fucked-up face
in 1953, when *Niagara* was the film
forbidden to us catholic kids.

use two different photos,
one from the final days,
if you want to show her decline,
what time and our own indulgences
do to us,
but don't lie with silkscreen;
don't employ the tricks you learned
in commercial art to reverse the process
and deglamorize.

let us enjoy a little beauty
while it lasts, while WE do.

we don't need another steenking
mememto mori.

claes oldenburg:
french fries and ketchup, giant fagends, and soft toilet

high concept and well
executed from materials
as close to hand as the
ingredients of alice waters'
cooking...

but...
i wouldn't want to eat them,
smoke them,
sit on it.

in fact, i hope i never even
look at them again.

robert therrien:
no title (blue plastic plates)

a stack of blue plates, saucers, bowls,
all a-kilter but balanced around
a central axis.
in spaghetti westerns they call
that masked man *contrapposto*.

it's a sculpture and
you walk around it.

the museum curator points out
the domesticity of the subject
in contract to the phallic assertiveness
of modernists like pollock and picasso.

still, bloomsbury was modernism also,
and largely bisexual,
and over at the huntington the exhibit
of roger fry, vanessa bell, and duncan grant
highlights the homespun,
still lifes of the familiar,
portraits of intimates informally posed,
gardens seen through windows,
the folding screens and other furniture
of the omega workshops.

plates also,
some white, some blue.
the soup bowls are capacious
as the tureens.
i hope they weren't ladled shallowly.
i just read in miss manners that
it's perfectly all right to lift
your bowl and drink from it.

THIS MARRIAGE OF MAN THE MAKER AND MOTHER NATURE

i've been doing that for years anyway,
because i love soups
and don't believe in waste.

waitresses and waiters know the art
of stacking kitchenware.
some women also, at the kitchen sink,
and more men than you'd think,
even in the old days.
i was never any good at it.
everything that i touch breaks.
so i eat out a lot.

"buffalo china,"
cheap and unpretentious,
good enough for me.

i started out suspicious of this piece,
but it kind of grows on you,
like campbell's soups or heinz.
that doesn't mean i'm about
to offer to help with household chores.
i think we men have been sufficiently
tamed, trained, restrained, and constrained
for the time being
(maybe even shackled).
i think i'll search the other wings
of this joint for a thrower of javelins,
hurler of thunderbolts,
moses, david, balzac,
pugilist or frontier lawman,
satyr.

Roy Lichtenstein: *Cold Shoulder*, circa 1963

A frigid greeting;
A balloon dripping icicles

Pampered prettiness
Dispenses instant chill

Lesson: Do not seek the sought-after.
Aspire to be the sought-after.

Jeff Koons: *Michael Jackson and Bubbles*

A society gets
The Celebrities and Simians
It does not ignore.

Andy Warhol: *Campbell's Soup Can*, **1964**

Things to notice:

The fleur-de-lis fringe.
The regal seal.
That the soup is tomato
(you paint TOMAHTO).
That it is "condensed"
The cyberspacial variety of the typefaces.

That the can is unopened.
That it will always be.

That we do not know
If any soup is in it.

That we view it from above.

That it curtseys to us.

That the apostrophe has been preserved.

THIS MARRIAGE OF MAN THE MAKER AND MOTHER NATURE

Roy Lichtenstein: *Brushstroke in Flight*, **1983**

Ahah! A Gesture that I haven't seen
A hundred times before: What a novelty!
Not a drip, a smudge, a slash, or shot-put,
Though maybe suggesting a smidgeon
Of one or two of these.

But more like the semi-schemed and
Semi-improvised thrust of the winning
Rapier in an Olympic event
Staged at MOMA.

If, that is, the colors were Red,
Blue, Yellow, and White.

Unless White should be dubbed
None of the Above.

An only slightly random and
Disjointed twisting of the elbow,
A temporary separation/restoration
Of the fencer's rotator cuff.

This kinesthetic second-nature
Runs to the essence of Mind-Body
Sex and Spontaneity.

Thanks, Roy.

ed ruscha
hollywood, 1968

the hollywood sign on the horizon.
sunset behind the hollywood hills
a sky at the infra-red end
of the cinematic spectrum.
the oblong dimensions of cinemascope,
even the illusion of depth
from the gradual foregrounding
of the latter letters.

you hear the hollywood bowl.
you sense the spirit of james dean.
mullholland murders and machinations
flicker in the noir beyond the frame,
the roar of road-rage
through the cahuenga pass.
you see why they named that crosstown artery
sunset boulevard.

but all of l.a. is excluded, wisely,
save this marriage of
man the maker and mother nature

Roy Lichtenstein: *Sleeping Muse*, **1983**

Until I read in the catalog
That it combined carving, welding,
Line, and Logo,

I just assumed it was
An inane
(to Brancusi)
Homage.

Now I'm afraid Henry Cooper
Is some kind of genius,

And that I've never learned more
From fewer words.

Wayne Thiebaud
FOOD BOWLS
New Yorker Cover

The farthest seems to hold a cone
Of mustard-mayonnaise potato salad,
Ringed by yolk-white slices of boiled egg,
Topped by a black maraschino olive,
Just the way my aunts
Stirred summer supper sustenance from it,
Served with fresh squeezed lemonade.

In one a ladle sunk into a salad,
Toss and swirl of lettuce, olive, and tomato.
Pepper, Pickle? Pickled peppers?
Swimming in oil, vinegar and herbs?

The third's a whipped dessert:
Strawberry? Egg whites? Whipping Cream?

The fourth one must be either mine or his:
Already empty/not yet filled?

Every artist is a starving artist.

ROY LICHTENSTEIN:
I...I'M SORRY,
1965-66

she means it, she is sorry,
truly sorry, unqualifiedly so,
without reservation or dissimulation.

her face--her surface--is all there is.
the face, the façade, is the fact.
there are no hidden depths,
no secret complicating self-reflections or
reflexivities, no lacanian subject-object
dualities, no derridean decentering
of the self.

the image is unitary.
the tear is as real as an
only semi-representational
image/tear can be.

i do not mean that the girls in the cartoons
of which she is a parody are necessarily
portrayed as truly sorry.

i don't mean that women in "real life"
ever really unalloyedly are,
or ever were.

i just mean that she is,
and i sure wish i knew
what she is sorry for,
so i could assure her of my
unmitigated forgiveness,

but maybe a sort of blanket papal
absolution will do, a kind of all-purpose
presidential pardon like the one that Nixon
got and clinton didn't.

edward ruscha
double standard, 1969

okay, so it's a stylized monumental pun,
two stylized gas signs,
white on brown and,
even larger, white on blue,
perpendicular to each other
above the cinematically flat station,
pumps with pumpkin faces
standing guard out front.

i'll take it as a tribute
to the dear old sociobiologically successful
sexual double standard:
what got us here--
to this evolutionary moment--
is what will keep us here...
although it is ominously dated
just about the time the women's movement
left the launching pad.

and new fangled technology be damned,
especially in the event of nuclear war,
drug-resistant bacteria, collision with
meteor, global warming, global
cooling, or global anything,
we may find ourselves back on that primitive
desert island that satirists such as j.m. barrie
and lena wertmuller are wont to imagine.

any irony intended by the artist,
i will simply willfully ignore.

and anyway i mainly like
to look at it:
an aesthetic artifact of planes
directions, tensions, textures,
and chromatic shadings, shadowings.

THIS MARRIAGE OF MAN THE MAKER AND MOTHER NATURE

something about it
(or about me)
makes me love america,
the world,
and adolescence.

jeff koons: *the new*, 1981-1987

somehow i don't think my wife would want
me to drag her to a series of installations
of vacuum cleaners.

andy warhol: *mao*, 1979

napoleon as a pop icon?
the moustache on the mona lisa?
a mere appropriation of the historical,
the seemingly meaningful,
into fabrication of design,
commercial image, coin of the realm?

or just a tribute to a
super-duper-celebrity whose fame outlasted
his allotted fifteen minutes?

i doubt that andy thought about it
at great length.
i think his art was instinct.
i think the rest of us
were thinking all too much
in those days,
maybe still,
and we loved andy for not thinking
for us or himself.

it was enough he saw things
and got us to take
a second look
(or twenty).

VI

THE REDUCTIVE

beyond geometry, but not very

joseph albers painted over 1000
"platters of color,"
in his homage to the square series.
i too believe in lifelong commitments
to serial/repetitive art projects,
and i add the dimension of incorporation
into everyday life and the kinetic interplay
of art-work, artist, and the body politic.

thus, i am already working on the consumption
and processing of the 10,000th consecutive
daily Gardenburger Combination Special
(with curly cajun fries, side salad, diet
pepsi),

and, to remove any suspicion of mercenary
capitalistic motivation, i am keeping no
videotape or other permanent and potentially
marketable record of my conceptual (though
certainly not trivial) achievement.

(borges would have appreciated me,
you effing philistines!)

Minimal Affirmative

i'm reading in a british book on contemporary
literature a chapter entitled "minimal
affirmation,"
which tried to microscopically locate the barely
visible ways in which we

bored betrayed despairing disenchanted
defrocked alienated fragmented impotent
uprooted nihilistic dissipated dissociated
defeatist defeated and indisputably MINOR

writers of the generations since WWII

have conspired to burp forth a barely audible
yea,
and i have to run off to give
a poetry reading,
and afterwards, of course, we all congregate
at the reno room to get drunk,

and someone asks me what it was like
teaching college in the 1960s
and without a second thought
i blurt out the eminently un-ennui-like,
"it...was...

JUST FUCKING GREAT!!!"

agnes martin: *the sea*, 2003

a square sea.
a sea squarely framed.
a sea without waves.
a sea of static.
a clueless, blueless sea.
and anti-sea.
a sea of grammared pain.

columbus could have said,
"you sea? i saw a sea
that you can't see
down by the see-saw."

jesus rafael soto:
almost immaterial vibration, **1963,**
wood, wire, and paint.

susan sontag sure nailed "op" and "pop" art early-on
in against interpretation, how there was no way to
interpret the first because it had no content
and the second (e.g. andy's soup cans)
because the apparent content was reduced
to pure repetitive form.

if you read french and split time between paris
and new york city, you catch on quicker to those
things.

you could also say they legislate against
looking and
against enjoyment: "pop" quickly sates, and "op"
makes you dizzy, gives you migraines.

both give you something to think about though,

for about five minutes,

once a decade.

blinky palermo:
softspeaker, **1965**

i'm not going to make any jokes
about this guy's overly obvious
art objects,

because i'm pretty sure i saw him
slinking around on the sopranos.

Anthony Caro: *Table Piece LXX*, 1968

A blacksmith's table setting.

Why waste perfectly good,

And otherwise useless,

Steel.

THIS MARRIAGE OF MAN THE MAKER AND MOTHER NATURE

cildo meireles:
***the southern cross**, 1969-70, (refabrication)*

not even a single silly centimeter,
this minor mass of fused surfaces may,
the brochure suggests, make me aware of
my largeness in comparison to some things,
my smallness in relation to others,
the largeness of the little cube
in comparison to some things (an electron?),
its smallness in relation to others (me?),
and the disproportionate hegemony of euro-
american cultural centers compared to, say,
those of brazil.

mainly, though, it reminds me of the
barricini's miniature chocolates that you used
to have to go to new york city to purchase
when i was a kid growing up upstate and
having to settle for the lumpen productions
of ms. fannie farmer, whereas the
metropolitan

confections were as exquisitely yin-yang in
their balancing of light and dark brown textures,
appearances, and tastes, as the "soft pines and
hard oaks" of this inspired little gem.

jan dibbetts:
***shortest day at the guggenheim museum new york 1970 from sunrise to midday photographed every five minutes*, 1970**

yeah, i'd never noticed that days usually get gradually
brighter in the morning. i'll be sure to pay greater attention from now on. but where's ed ruscha when we really need to lighten up a little?

Robert Smithson:
Spiral Jetty, 1970

I've never seen it but,
In *The New Yorker* photo by Tom Smart,
It is a thing of alkaline and geologic beauty,
Bulldozers the artist's brush and chisel,
And, like Steven's jar in Tennessee,
It brings order, focus, to the one-dimensionality
Of glare.

I've inhaled the acrid sushi of decay,
Fled the plague of sand fleas,
Been blinded by its Gnostic gloom,
Sought whisky to wash down beef jerky.

The Mormons stared it in the eye,
And ever since have clung together.

But the jetty--Spiral nebula--upon which treads
The French Lieutenant's Woman,
Revenant in shawl upon Lyme Regi's mole--

With all the ugliness inflicted upon nature,
Perhaps we'll be forgiven humanizing it a tad
At its most inhumane.

mel bochner:
continous/dis/continuous, 1971-72

black clockwise squares of numbers
alternate with red counterclockwise
squares of numbers.

why?

that's what we're supposed to
ask ourselves, dummy!

but why we need to ask ourselves:
that will take a more inquiring mind
than mine to figure out.

stanislaw drozdz:
miedzy **(between), 1977 (reconstruction)**

"ephemeral installation: letters of the
polish word miedzy
("between") painted systematically in black
on the floor,
being, and walls of a white room."

i couldn't have said it better myself.
but it didn't really make me "hear" the word
between
(and i wouldn't recognize the polish word
if i did hear it), nor did i feel myself
between
"word and meaning, language and image,
art and everyday life."

there's a point at which defamiliarization is
either counterproductive or just simply
doesn't work,
as when you begin to mistake garden hoses
for boa
constrictors or cease to give a flying fig
newton
about either.

richard serra: *switch*

will we build within buildings?
will our parks be planes of rust?
will we torque our walls into
the a-symmetrical to keep our minds
from going blank with sameness?
will we construct abstract yosemites,
grand canyons of inverted cones?
will we wander arbitrary alleyways
and never wonder why?
will we delight in warp?

is the ellipsis the shape
of sleep to come?

worship the gray eel.
eat the oblong wafer without salt.
fail to remember madrigals.
chew metal.

agnes martin: *homage to life*, **2003**

at 92 she knows both life and death
are black.
black is all temperatures from the
bizarre to blank.
blood is black; breath is black
black is trapezoidal,
both the pit and the pyramid,
the trapdoor and the pedestal.
a miniskirt is trapezoidal,
and a pulpit adenoidal.

square is to trapezoid
as aether is to onyx,
grid to squid,
blotch to sasquatch.

and if i live another thirty years
(and she has)
there is just no telling how profound
i'll have become.
i may, for instance, have intuited
that white is all temperatures
from pissarro to mel blanc.

VII

THE PAINTERS

chuck close

i paint portraits because
faces do not interest me.
i paint the unimportant.
i organize the organic into
inorganic grids. i look at
life through a screen door,
and i want you to.

RICHARD DIEBENKORN: *Girl Smoking*

elegant legs, gracefully crossed.
not hopper's pallet, but
a diva on a divan,
knowing she's attractive
but without illusions of divinity:
thus not a prima donna.

vulnerable shoulders.
a nipple out of nowhere.
she hugs herself, supports
an elbow on a forearm.

anxiety as well as inhalation.
sophistication, but not
ellington exactly either.
the room an atmosphere of color
...and cologne?

home from the dance?
home from the date?
home from the cabaret?

a lady in waiting,
wondering if he will show?
we used to be able to feel good
about the way we smoked,
the way we looked when smoking.
it was theatre.
a lot of women that I dated
used to smoke. after sex,
a cigarette, a drink,
pleasure after pleasure,
sitting up in bed,
or at a kitchen table.
killing time until the next time.
friendly conversations,
with each other, with ourselves.

THIS MARRIAGE OF MAN THE MAKER AND MOTHER NATURE

they write me sometimes,
now married with grown children,
spacious homes and gardens,
justly proud and doting husbands.

good times, they say;
we had good times.

they *were* good times.

they say, i don't know if
you will remember me.

yes, yes, i do.
now more than ever,
after thirty or more years

a sketch,
a smoky reverie of red coiffure
a femininity gone out of fashion

yes, yes, they were the best of times,
though perilous, now proved imperishable.

my god i'm glad that i have
women to remember
and that to some at least
i meant good times

Willem de Kooning: *Untitled,* **1976-7**
and
Roy Lichtenstein:
Painting with Statue of Liberty, **1985**

Otto Jespersen deduced
That Metaphor and Metonymy
In excess, unbridled,

Yield Schizophrenia and Paranoia,

A crucifixion upon the horizontal axis
Of Contiguity, or the Vertical axis
Of Substitutions.

In other words, in the Art World,
If you ain't the Mad Hatter,
You're probably the Cheshire Cat.

muna kata shiko:
a self-portrait with joy, **1963**

lots to look at in
this colored woodcut:

creativity, sex, cacti,
cooking, travel flowers,
cigarettes, stars, and tradition.

all the accoutrements of
one man's life and work.

the symbols/cymbals do indeed
strike sparks and clangs of joy
against each other.

i also notice several sake bowls.

maurice denis:
portrait of marthe denis, the artist's wife,
1983

this guy sure had the hots
for his wife, and why not?
all that roundness of face,
arms, and bosom. The way
she adjusts the shoulder strap
of the garment that barely
hides her nipples, the freshness
of her youthful flesh. her
willingness yet coquetry

the rest of life is laundry,
fences, commerce, weather,
and foreboding forestry.
best to, as long as possible,
extend the honeymoon.
best to bury one's face
against her breasts,
between her thighs.

JASPER JOHNS:
FOUR *UNTITLED* WORKS:
1975, -84, -91, -91-94

you realize there's more than meets the eye,
sub-strata that pop art is not supposed to
take an interest in. you have to *look* more
than my aging orbs are used to doing or
can do without discomfort. you'll find
ambiguous shapes, shadows, circuitries,
eyes looking back at you. words out of
context, meltings, brush-strokes at cross-
purposes, fading recollections, precarious
salvagings, the contexts of the patterns that
may be from dream, from childhood, or
the psych-sexual history of the human race.

or maybe we still mourn the angst of the
amoeba, rent beyond self-love.

basquiat and jasper johns: cave-painters on
the communal membranes of the skull.

RICHARD DIEBENKORN: *Untitled, 1992*

ah yes, unaddressed also:
a white envelope, of course.

but a yellow envelope? well,
why not--to post bad news to
cockeyed optimists, perhaps.

patches within patches,
patches upon patches.
as enigmatic and unsignifying
as the harlequin man happily inhabiting
the heart of darkness

envelopes unstuffed, the perfectly
unsignifying signifiers.
or maybe signifying everything.
we try so desperately to invest
our circumambient rectangularity
with interest, maybe even beauty.

slicing into triangles,
tearing off the corners,
inventing ever more shades and hybrids
for our crayon box.

an envelope that doesn't open,
flat,
unaddressed to all of us.

THIS MARRIAGE OF MAN THE MAKER AND MOTHER NATURE

joan mitchell: *l'arbre de phyllis*, **1991**

this painting wore khakis.
this painting wore fatigues.
this painting was a parade,
the easter of the risen daffodil,
the loam of graves and forests,
the white of sacrificial wool,
of pasty, leprous lazarus,
of pearly gates,
and of a tom wolfe palm beach suit.

our aging urine drips and
stains our droopy drawers,

but at the end
a something rises,

as the martyred blackrobe
and his huron surgeon

witnessed in astonishment.

the joke is on the would-be murderer
and even on the art that thinks
it has outgrown it.

de kooning in dementia

we love who we were.
failing memory delineates
with fewer lines.
we add primary colors, happier ones,
because we are less happy now than
when we thought ourselves so tortured.
we emulate the cartoons of childhood.
every day we awake to saturday morning.
we replace the hormones with harmony,
filter the acidulous from sex.
we give up the game,
retain the play.
we draw with broken strokes and
speak a lexicon of fewer words.
we do not articulate ideas.
we forget our fetishes;
we forgive poor, silly lucifer.
we are what we were
before we were.

for a while there everything
got so damn complicated that
we just went nuts.
now we are returning to
that simpler place, that womb
where we will be
one with the view.

happy mother's day.

THIS MARRIAGE OF MAN THE MAKER AND MOTHER NATURE

ABOUT THE AUTHOR

Almost every one of his published books mentions where he taught and for how long and gives the large number of books he wrote, so here is something else about the author: Like Jack Nicholson, he is a dedicated fan of the New York Yankees and the Los Angeles Lakers.

PUBLISHERS'S NOTE

For many years Gerald Locklin had his poetry about art published in *Coagula Art Journal*. This is the second and final volume bringing all of those poems together. It was a fantastic collaboration.
--Mat Gleason, September 2014

Made in the USA
Middletown, DE
23 February 2015